Disabilities and Differences

We All Communicate

Rebecca Rissman

Heinemann Library
Chicago, Illinois

Customer Service 888-454-2279
Visit our website at www.heinemannlibrary.com

Printed in China by South China Printing Company Limited

13 12 11 10 09
10 9 8 7 6 5 4 3 2 1

Library of Congress Cataloging-in-Publication Data
Rissman, Rebecca.
  We all communicate / Rebecca Rissman.
     p. cm. -- (Disabilities and differences)
  Includes bibliographical references and index.
  ISBN 978-1-4329-2152-1 (hc) -- ISBN 978-1-4329-2158-3 (pb) 1. Interpersonal communication--Juvenile literature. I. Title.
  HM1166.R57 2008
  302.2--dc22
                              2008029746

Acknowledgments
The author and publisher are grateful to the following for permission to reproduce photographs: ©agefotostock pp. 16 (Image Source/Royalty Free), 20 (John Birdsall); ©drr.net pp. 10 (Borut Peterlin), 11 (Huntstock.com), 14 (enzodalverme.com), 15 (Image Source Ltd.), 23 bottom (enzodalverme.com); ©Getty Images pp. 4 (Ryan McVay), 7 (Chris Cheadle), 9 (David Deas), 13 (Paul Viant), 19 (Jacobs Stock Photography); ©Heinemann Raintree p. 6 (Richard Hutchings); ©istockphoto p. 17 (ranplett); ©Jupiter Images p. 21 (Comma Image); ©PhotoEdit pp. 22 (Michael Newman), 23 middle (Michael Newman); ©Shutterstock pp. 8 (Amra Pasic), 12 (Ronen), 23 top (Ronen).

Cover image used with permission of ©AP Photo (Mahesh Kumar A). Back cover image used with permission of ©Shutterstock (Rob Marmion).

Every effort has been made to contact copyright holders of any material reproduced in this book. Any omissions will be rectified in subsequent printings if notice is given to the publisher.

Contents

Differences

4

We are all different.

Communicating

People communicate in different ways.

People understand in different ways.

Listening

Some people listen to loud sounds.

Some people listen to quiet sounds.

Some people listen to a teacher.

Some people listen to a friend.

headphones

Some people listen to a television.

Some people listen to a radio.

Talking

People talk in different ways.

People talk in different places.

15

Some people talk in loud voices.

Some people talk in soft voices.

Some people talk to their family.

Some people talk to their neighbor.

Some people talk on the telephone.

Some people talk on the computer.

We Are All Different

We are all different.

How do you talk? How do you listen?

Words to Know

 **headphones** small speakers worn over the ears. Headphones help people hear.

 **hearing aid** small machine that helps people hear. Hearing aids fit inside the ear.

 **sign language** way to communicate with hand signs

This section includes related vocabulary words that can help students learn about this topic. Use these words to explore communication.

Index

Note to Parents and Teachers
Before reading
Encourage students to think of the ways that they are different from one another. Then explain that being different makes everyone special.

After reading
Ask children to list as many ways to communicate as they can think of (e.g., writing emails, talking on the telephone, sign language). Then, have students vote on their favorite way to communicate and record the answers on the board.